For My Daughter

From Your Mother

IF ANY ONE FACULTY OF OUR NATURE MAY BE CALLED MORE WONDERFUL THAN THE REST, I DO THINK IT IS MEMORY.
—JANE AUSTEN

Louis Weber, CEO
Publications International, Ltd.
7373 North Cicero Avenue
Lincolnwood, Illinois 60712

www.pilbooks.com

Manufactured in China.

8 7 6 5 4 3 2 1

ISBN-13: 978-1-4508-7041-2
ISBN-10: 1-4508-7041-4

Dear Daughter

MY THOUGHTS
AND MEMORIES OF YOU

new seasons®

THE DAY YOU WERE BORN...

MY NEWBORN BABY

WHEN YOU FIRST STARTED SPEAKING, I KNEW...

The most interesting information comes from children, for they tell all they know.

— MARK TWAIN

MY FAVORITE BABY STORY ABOUT YOU...

MY BABY GIRL

YOUR IMAGINATION HAS ALWAYS BEEN...

I DISTINCTLY REMEMBER WORKING ON THIS PROJECT WITH YOU...

I LOVED, AND STILL ENJOY, WATCHING YOU AND YOUR SIBLINGS...

KIDS WILL BE KIDS

A STORY ABOUT YOU AND AN ANIMAL THAT YOU LOVED...

The dog was created specially for children. He is the god of frolic.

— HENRY WARD BEECHER

A PRICELESS STORY ABOUT YOU AND YOUR CHILDHOOD FRIENDS...

BEST FRIENDS

A BOOK WE LOVED TO READ AND DISCUSS...

It is only a novel...or in short, only some work in which the greatest powers of the mind are displayed, in which the most thorough knowledge of human nature, the happiest delineation of its varieties, the liveliest effusions of wit and humor are conveyed to the world in the best-chosen language.

— JANE AUSTEN

A TEACHER'S PRAISE I'LL NEVER FORGET...

A CLASS ACT

YOU WERE ALWAYS THE CENTER OF ATTENTION, AND STILL ARE, WHEN IT COMES TO... ____________

WHEN OUR WHOLE FAMILY GETS TOGETHER,

I LOVE SEEING YOU...

I THINK YOUR RELATIONSHIP WITH YOUR GRANDPARENTS...

FAMILY LOVE

OUR HOLIDAY TRADITIONS, THEN AND NOW...

I THINK MY FAVORITE TIME OF YEAR TO SPEND WITH YOU IS... ____________

YOUR CHILDHOOD BIRTHDAYS WERE SO SPECIAL TO ME BECAUSE...

Youth is happy because it has the ability to see beauty. Anyone who keeps the ability to see beauty never grows old.

— FRANZ KAFKA

A BIRTHDAY GIFT YOU GAVE ME THAT STILL MEANS SO MUCH...

A BIRTHDAY TRADITION I HOPE YOU HAVE WITH YOUR CHILDREN...

ONE OF MY FAVORITE VACATIONS WITH YOU...

Traveling in the company
of those we love is
home in motion.

— JAMES HENRY LEIGH HUNT

A SPECIAL MEMORY I HAVE OF YOU DURING YOUR TEEN YEARS...

SOMETHING YOU ACCOMPLISHED AT A YOUNG AGE THAT SO IMPRESSED ME...

A TIME I THOUGHT YOU WERE VERY WISE...

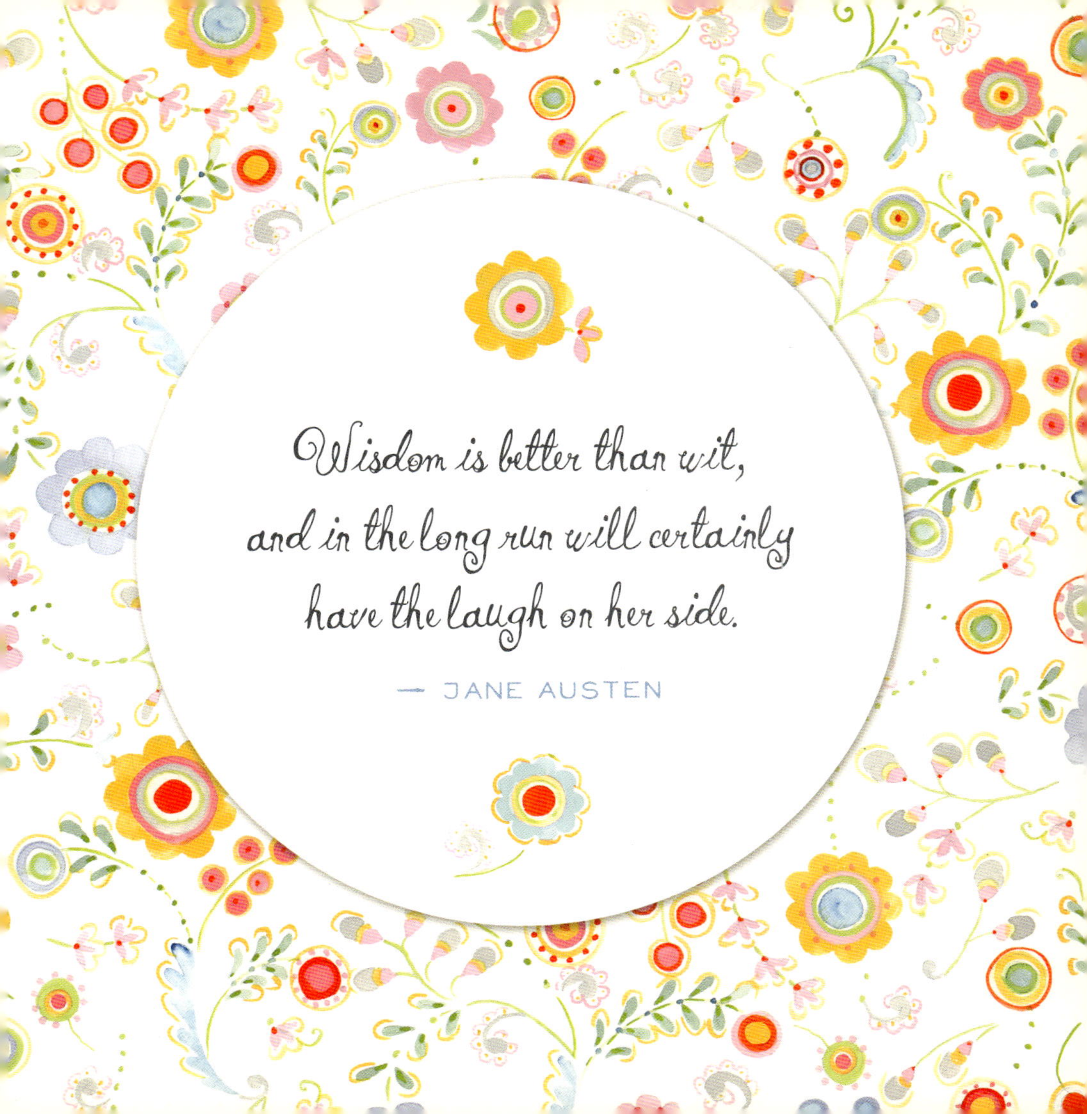
Wisdom is better than wit,
and in the long run will certainly
have the laugh on her side.
— JANE AUSTEN

WHEN YOU STARTED DRIVING, I WAS...

YOUR FIRST CAR

YOU WERE SO INSPIRED BY THIS PERSON...

YOU INSPIRE ME TO...

MUSIC I STILL LOVE TO LISTEN TO WITH YOU...

Music is the
shorthand of emotion.
— LEO TOLSTOY

AS YOU MATURED, I SAW YOUR CONFIDENCE...

YOU WERE MUCH BRAVER THAN I WAS WHEN IT CAME TO...

I REMEMBER YOUR FIRST CRUSH...

The very essence of romance is uncertainty.

— OSCAR WILDE

HELPING YOU GET READY FOR YOUR SCHOOL DANCES...

BEAUTY QUEEN

WATCHING YOU GET READY FOR DATES DURING YOUR TEEN YEARS...

OUR DISCUSSIONS ABOUT DATING WHEN YOU WERE OLDER...

SOME ADVICE I WISH I HAD GIVEN YOU...

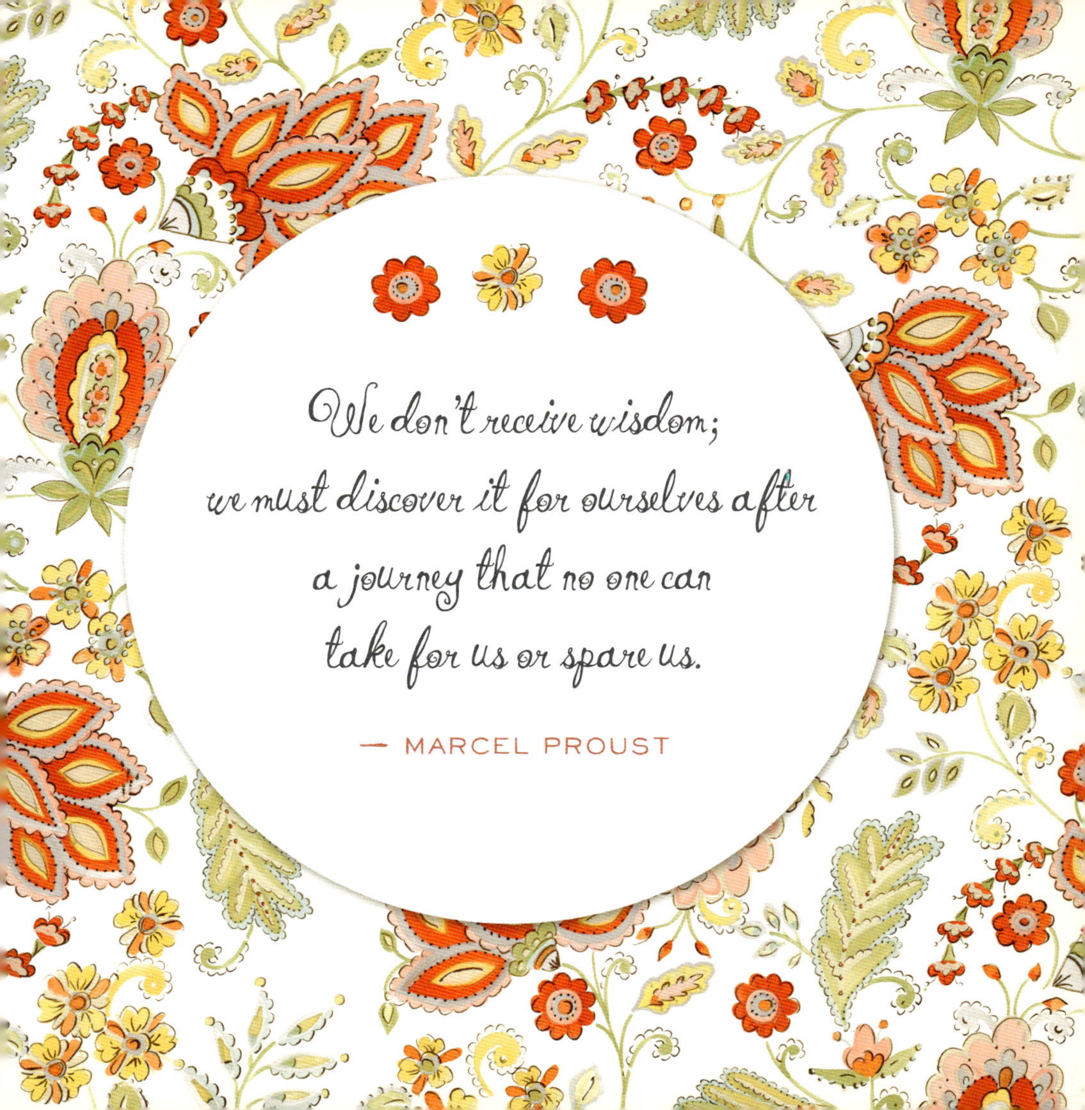
We don't receive wisdom;
we must discover it for ourselves after
a journey that no one can
take for us or spare us.
— MARCEL PROUST

I KNEW YOU WERE REALLY IN LOVE WHEN...

YOUR FIRST HEARTBREAK...

WHEN THE TIME GREW NEAR FOR YOU TO LEAVE HOME...

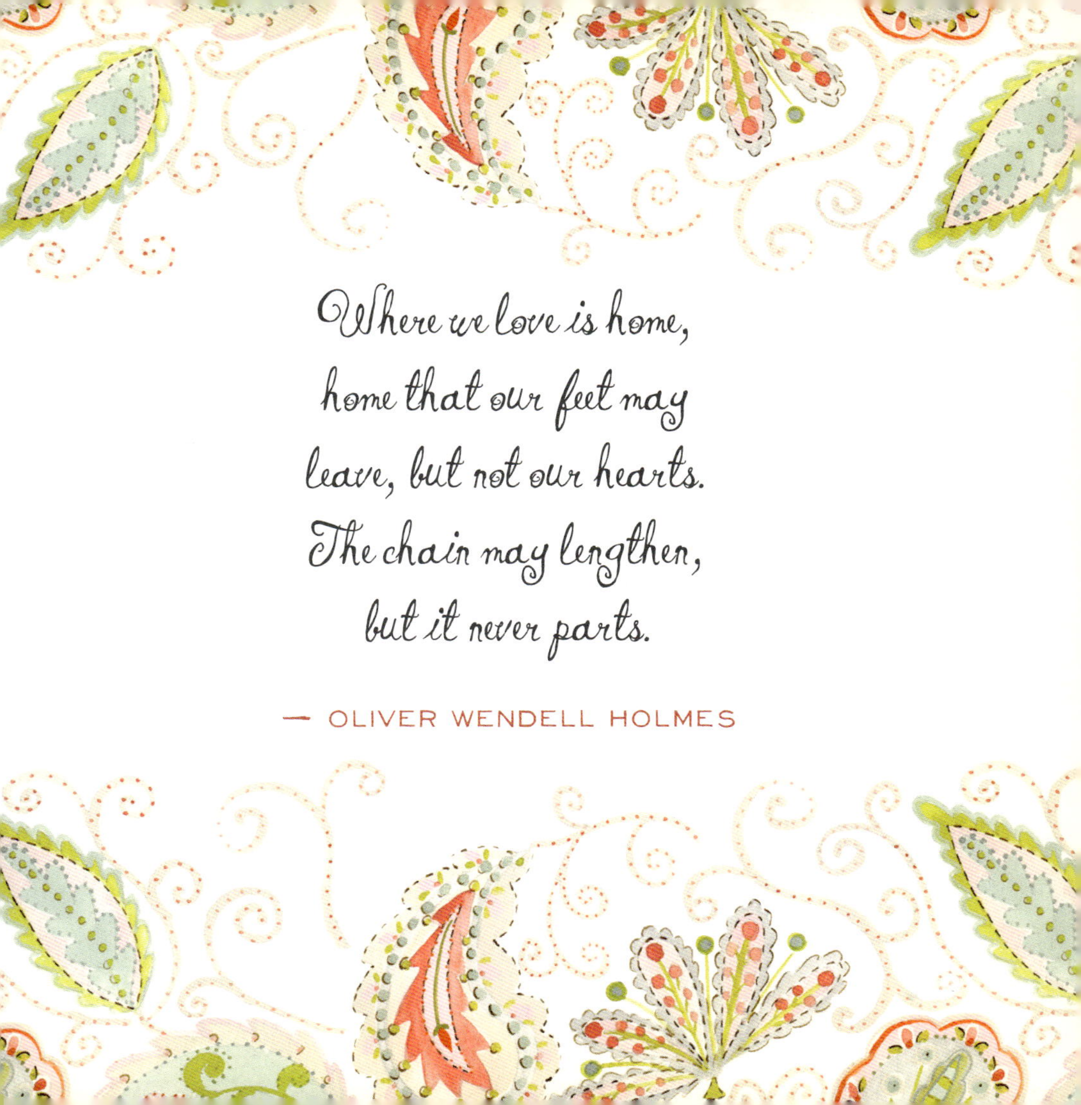

Where we love is home,
home that our feet may
leave, but not our hearts.
The chain may lengthen,
but it never parts.

— OLIVER WENDELL HOLMES

A GREAT COLLEGE VISIT WE HAD TOGETHER...

I KNEW WE HAD FOUND THE SCHOOL FOR YOU WHEN...

DURING YOUR FIRST YEARS AWAY FROM HOME, OUR RELATIONSHIP GREW AND CHANGED...

AN OCCASION WHEN I WANTED TO LIVE VICARIOUSLY THROUGH YOU...

NOW THAT YOU ARE AN ADULT, I CHERISH OUR TALKS BECAUSE...

A SPECIAL MOMENT

I REMEMBER YOUR FIRST BIG JOB INTERVIEW...

I KNEW YOU HAD FOUND YOUR CALLING...

THROUGHOUT YOUR PROFESSIONAL CAREER, I HOPE YOU WILL...

The secret to getting ahead
is getting started.
— MARK TWAIN

WHEN YOU TOLD ME YOU HAD FOUND THE PERSON YOU WANTED TO SPEND THE REST OF YOUR LIFE WITH...

I KNEW YOU WOULD FIND HAPPINESS...

ON YOUR BIG DAY, I WAS OVERCOME WITH EMOTION, BUT WHAT I REMEMBER MOST...

MOTHER & BRIDE

FROM ONE MOTHER TO ANOTHER, I WANT YOU TO KNOW...

MY BEST ADVICE FOR A SUCCESSFUL PARENT-CHILD RELATIONSHIP...

YOU ARE SUCH A GIFT TO ME BECAUSE...

*A daughter is a little girl
who grows up to be a friend.*

— ANONYMOUS